TAE KWON DO

NEIL MORRIS

HEINEMANN LIBRARY
CHICAGO, ILLINOIS

© 2001 Reed Educational & Professional Publishing
Published by Heinemann Library,
an imprint of Reed Educational & Professional Publishing,
Chicago, Illinois

Customer Service 888-454-2279

Visit our website at www.heinemannlibrary.com

Designed by Ken Vail Graphic Design, Cambridge
Illustrations by Simon Girling & Associates (Mike Lacey)
Originated by Dot Gradations
Printed by Wing King Tong in Hong Kong.

05 04 03 02 01
10 9 8 7 6 5 4 3 2 1

Library of Congress Cataloging-in-Publication Data
Morris, Neil, 1946-
   Tae kwon do / Neil Morris.
      p. cm. -- (Get going! Martial arts)
Includes bibliographical references (p.) and index.
   ISBN 1-58810-041-3
   1. Tae kwon do--Juvenile literature. [1. Tae kwon do.] I. Title.
   GV1114.9 .M67 2001
   796.815'3--dc21
                                    00-013196

Acknowledgments
The Publishers would like to thank the following for permission to reproduce photographs: Blitz, p. 9; Sylvio Dokov, p. 29; European Press Agency/P. A. News, pp. 4, 25; Fiona Hanson, p. 5; Mark Hupton, p. 6; Rex Features, p. 7. All other photographs by Trevor Clifford.

Cover photograph reproduced with permission of P. A. News.

The Publisher would like to thank Master Reneé Sereff, of the United States Taekwon-Do Federation, for helping us improve the accuracy of this text.

Some words are shown in bold, **like this.** You can find out what they mean by looking in the glossary.

Korean words are shown in italics, *like this.* You can find out what they mean by looking at the chart on page 30.

CONTENTS

! Please remember that martial arts need to be taught by a qualified, registered teacher. Do not try any of the techniques and movements in this book without such an instructor present.

WHAT IS TAE KWON DO?

Tae kwon do is a Korean martial art that is practiced by 50 million people throughout the world. Its name means "way of the foot and the fist." Tae kwon do is best known for its use of spectacular flying kicks. It is sometimes called kick-boxing, but this is not a term that martial artists use for the sport. Tae kwon do combines some of the movements from Japanese **karate** and Chinese **kung fu.**

Like other martial arts, tae kwon do offers students the opportunity to take part in a competitive sport, practice demanding physical routines, and learn about self-defense. It is based on strong mental discipline, and it teaches students to do things correctly, demonstrating self-control and respect for others.

Top-level tae kwon do competitors demonstrate the exciting sport.

AN OLYMPIC SPORT

At the Olympic Games held in Sydney, Australia, in 2000, tae kwon do became the second martial art to be accepted as an Olympic sport. **Judo** was first seen at the Tokyo Olympics in 1964. In Sydney, 52 men and 48 women competed for gold medals in tae kwon do.

The Olympic form of the sport follows the rules laid down by the World Taekwondo Federation. All competitors must wear protective gear, and full-contact kicks and punches are made to specific target areas. By contrast, the form of the sport promoted by the International Taekwondo Federation allows only light contact.

WHERE TO LEARN AND PRACTICE

This book tells you how to get started in tae kwon do. It also shows and explains some tae kwon do techniques, so that you can understand and practice them. But you must always remember that you cannot learn a martial art just from a book. To be a serious student of tae kwon do, you must go to regular lessons with a qualified teacher, so that you learn all the techniques properly and then repeat and practice them many times.

Choose your club carefully. It should have an experienced teacher and it should belong to an approved national tae kwon do association. The list on page 31 shows where you can get information and lists of clubs.

Tae kwon do students in South Korea demonstrate their skills.

TAE KWON DO—THE BEGINNINGS

Tae kwon do is an ancient martial art. The oldest records are about 2,000 years old. They are from a period in Korean history known as the Three Kingdoms that began in 37 B.C.E. In an ancient royal tomb in one of the kingdoms, called Koguryo, wall paintings show unarmed fighters practicing techniques that are very similar to those of modern tae kwon do.

In another of the Three Kingdoms, called Silla, the young sons of nobles were taught to become strong warriors, and to be members of a group called the *hwarang,* meaning "flower of youth." A form of combat known as *taekkyon* was an important part of their training to become military leaders. It was seen as a way of building strength by using the hands and feet freely, and at the same time training the body to adapt to any danger or attack.

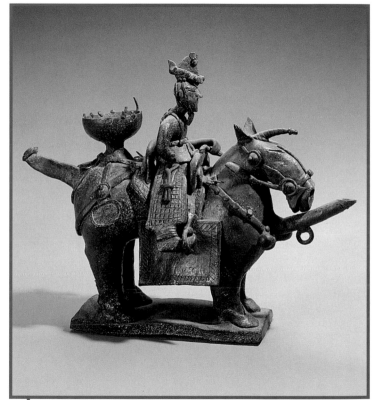

This stoneware model of a warrior on horseback was made in the ancient Korean kingdom of Silla.

This martial art was taught to go along with five principles for young warriors—to be loyal to their kingdom, to be obedient to their parents, to be trustworthy to their friends, to never retreat in battle, and to kill an enemy only when absolutely necessary.

FLYING KICKS

Traveling *hwarang* warriors spread the knowledge of their martial art, then known as *subak*. The flying kick techniques were probably developed to knock men off their horses. By the time of the Korean Yi dynasty, which ruled from 1392 to 1910, *subak* was taught more for health and fitness. Then, when the Japanese occupied Korea from 1910 to 1945, all Korean martial arts were banned.

In 1955, various Korean martial arts schools came together to agree on one style. Major-General Choi Hong Hi, a black belt martial artist, founded the agreed-upon style. Two years later, it was given the name *tae kwon do.* Study of the art spread quickly in Korean schools and colleges.

Tae kwon do students took part in the opening ceremony of the Seoul Olympics in 1988. Twelve years later, tae kwon do officially became an Olympic sport.

In 1973, the first world championships were held in Seoul, the capital of South Korea. Thirty countries took part in the tournament. Korea took first place, and representatives from all the countries founded the World Taekwondo Federation. Since then, the world championships have been held in countries all over the world, including the United States and Canada.

EQUIPMENT

Tae kwon do is practiced and performed in a special white outfit called a *dobok*. It is best to buy a *dobok* through your club, but you do not need one right away. For the first few sessions, a sweatshirt and sweatpants or a T-shirt and jogging pants should be fine. Check with your club first.

The *dobok* is all white, although versions approved by some tae kwon do organizations have a black trim for more advanced students. It is made up of a pair of trousers and a loose jacket tied at the waist with a belt. *Doboks* are usually sold with a white belt, which is the right color for a beginner. Make sure that your *dobok* is large enough so that your movements will not be limited in any way.

It is very important to treat your *dobok* with respect. It should always be clean, washed, and ironed. A neat and tidy appearance shows that you have the right attitude toward training. Inside the training hall or gymnasium, called a *dojang,* you must always have bare feet. A pair of flip-flops is useful to keep your feet clean as you walk from the changing room to the *dojang.*

PUTTING ON THE DOBOK

Put the trousers on first. Many *dobok* bottoms have elastic at the waist. If they have a drawstring, pull it and tie it in a bow. Next put on the jacket. Some jackets have a v-neck instead of an open front and are slipped on over the head.

This student is showing how to put on the dobok *top.*

1 To tie the belt, pull it across your stomach first, keeping the two ends equal.

2 Wrap the belt around your waist twice, starting from the front.

3 Cross the left end over the right, then pull it up behind both layers of the belt.

4 Finally, tie the free ends together right over left and pull them through to finish the knot. Make sure the two ends are equal in length.

 SAFETY

In order not to harm yourself or anyone else, do not wear a watch or any jewelry. Keep your fingernails and toenails trimmed short. Pull long hair back, but do not use metal clips.

Make sure that you are in good shape for active exercise, and do not train if you are ill. Exercise should not hurt, so never push yourself to a point at which you feel pain.

Any martial art can be dangerous if it is not performed properly. Never fool around inside or outside the training hall—or at home or in school—by showing off or pretending to have a real fight.

 PROTECTIVE EQUIPMENT

Headgear, mouthguards, and chest protectors should be worn when practicing any form of competition or **sparring.** Boys should wear protective cups. The amount of protection you wear will depend on the style your club follows.

IN THE DOJANG

It is important for all martial arts students to show respect to everyone and everything to do with their sport, including the training hall. When they go into the *dojang,* tae kwon do students bow to their instructor or to the **senior grade.** If there is no one in the *dojang* when you enter, stop inside the entrance and bow to the middle of the hall. Always do the same when you leave the hall. The tae kwon do bow is called *kyungye* in Korean.

MAKING A BOW

The *kyungye* is made before and after every exercise, as well as to an opponent before and after each contest. Students also bow when they pass equipment such as safety pads to each other.

To perform the bow, first put your heels and toes together and place your hands against the side of your thighs. Then bow smoothly by bending your upper body forward, but not too far. Bend your head down so that your eyes look downward. Count to two as you hold that position. Then straighten up again.

There is a saying that "tae kwon do begins and ends with courtesy."

This is how to sit when your instructor is talking to you.

THE RIGHT ATTITUDE

Courtesy is one of the five important principles that show that students have the right attitude toward tae kwon do. When your instructor is talking to you in the *dojang,* you should sit in a cross-legged position and listen carefully and politely. Remember that during a training session, students should never talk among themselves, fool around, or fidget.

The other principles are integrity, perseverance, self-control, and an indomitable spirit. Integrity means being honest, always doing your very best and not pretending or cheating. Perseverance means that you keep going and never give up, even when things get difficult. Self-control is essential in all martial arts. You must never lose your temper or get too **aggressive** with a fellow student or an opponent. Indomitable spirit means showing that you cannot be defeated by any difficulty.

WARMING UP

Tae kwon do involves hard, physical exercise. It is important to warm your body up and stretch your muscles before training so that you do not injure yourself. Always start a session with some warm-up exercises. Begin by walking or jogging in place for a couple of minutes, then do some stretching exercises.

STRETCHING EXERCISES

Try these exercises to stretch your muscles before starting to train.

WINDMILLS

Turn your arms like the sails of a windmill to warm up.

1 Stand up straight with your arms by your sides.

2 Swing your left arm forward, up, and around behind you in a circle. Keep your arm straight and reach high at the top of the circle. Repeat five times.

3 Do the same exercise with the right arm.

4 Repeat the exercise, this time swinging both arms at the same time.

UPPER BACK STRETCH

1 Stand up straight and clasp your hands together behind your back, locking your fingers together.

2 Lift your hands up as high as you can and as far away from your back as possible. Hold this position for a count of five. Then return to the starting position.

3 Repeat the exercise five times.

GLUTEAL STRETCH

The *gluteus maximus* is the formal name for the muscles in your buttocks—the largest muscles in the human body.

1 Stand up straight and raise your right knee. Lock your fingers together under the knee and hold this position for a count of ten.

2 Repeat the exercise with the left leg.

3 Repeat the whole exercise three times.

! IMPORTANT

● Drink a lot of water, and do not exercise too hard when it is very hot or humid.

● Never exercise when you are ill or injured.

● Try not to breathe too hard and fast when you are exercising or resting.

● Do not hold your breath while exercising.

● When you are stretching, you should always remain comfortable and your muscles should not hurt. If you feel pain, stop what you are doing.

● Begin to exercise immediately after you have warmed up. Do cool-down activities immediately after you exercise.

STANCES

As a tae kwon do student, you will have many basic techniques to learn before you can start to put moves together. There are four different sets of basic techniques, made up of **stances,** blocks, punches, and kicks.

In tae kwon do, stances are not just a way of standing. They are fighting positions that need to be learned and practiced. They form the beginning and the foundation of all the other techniques. Practicing them also helps to build up the right muscles and develop good balance. When advanced students are **sparring,** or tae kwon do competitors are actually fighting, the stances between moves are held for only a split second as the fighters flow from one technique to another.

READY STANCE

This first stance, called *choonbi* in Korean, is sometimes called the first or beginning position. When you stand in this way, it means you are ready to practice tae kwon do.

1 Stand with your feet a shoulder-width apart and your weight spread evenly between them.

2 Bring your fists in front of your chest and then lower them to your waist. Your knuckles should form a slight v-shape.

3 Keep looking straight ahead. This position is used at the start of all the **patterns** you will learn on pages 22–23.

WALKING STANCE

1 This stance, *apkoobi,* is a good starting point for front attacks and defenses.

2 Step forward on your right foot, with the front leg slightly bent and the back leg straight. Draw both fists up to your sides at waist level to be ready for the next movement.

L STANCE

1 This stance, *dwit koobi,* presents a small and difficult target to the opponent.

2 From the ready stance, step forward with your left foot, turning your body to the right and putting most of your weight on your back, right leg.

SITTING STANCE

1 It is easy to see why this is called the sitting stance, *choochoom soegi.* It is a strong position for attacking and defending to either side.

2 Spread your legs so your feet are one and one-half shoulder-widths apart. Bend your knees so that you are half-squatting. Keep your back straight.

3 Pull your fists back at waist level.

BLOCKING

In martial arts and other contact sports, players have to learn to defend themselves against attack. Blocks are especially important in tae kwon do, because they provide a form of self-defense. In competition, they stop the opponent from scoring. Most blocks are made with the arms and hands, though some are performed with the legs and feet. Blocks can be learned without an opponent or partner, and form part of many tae kwon do **patterns.**

DOWN BLOCK

The downward or low block, *arae makki,* is used against kicks and punches aimed at the lower body. It can be learned and practiced in the walking **stance.**

1 With your right foot forward, cross your right fist over your chest and bring it up to be near your left ear.

2 To make the down block against an imaginary opponent's arm or leg, sweep your right arm down in a circular movement across your body, blocking with the forearm. At the same time, put your left fist into position at waist level.

RISING BLOCK

The rising or upper block, *eolgol makki*, is a good defense against straight punches to the face and overhead attacks to the head. Like the down block, it is performed in the walking stance.

1 Put your right arm above your left shoulder. Move your left arm straight down toward your groin.

2 Sweep your left arm up, blocking with the outside of the forearm. At the same time, put your right fist into position at waist level.

INNER BLOCK

The inner or inside block, *momtong makki*, protects against straight attacks to the upper body.

1 With your left foot forward, raise both of your arms toward the left side of your head.

2 Then put your right fist in the usual position at waist level, and quickly move your left fist to block the strike.

KOREAN NUMBERS

In tae kwon do, counting is often done in Korean:

One	*hana*	Six	*yasot*
Two	*dul*	Seven	*elgub*
Three	*set*	Eight	*yodol*
Four	*net*	Nine	*ahob*
Five	*dasot*	Ten	*yol*

STRIKING

In tae kwon do, you can strike with your hands and arms in many different ways. One of the most important strikes is the straight punch. For this, it is important to make a fist correctly, so that your punch is as powerful as possible but does not hurt you, the striker. Power comes from having your fist, wrist, elbow, shoulder, and other parts of your body all acting together. You can practice punching against an opponent holding a pad.

MAKING A FIST

1 To make a fist, first fold your fingers down. Then fold your thumb across the index and middle fingers, to lock them in.

2 In a tae kwon do punch, you aim at the target with the first two knuckles. Keep your fist straight in line with your arm, so that the wrist does not bend when you hit the target. But make sure that your arm stays slightly bent when you punch, so as not to put too much strain on your elbow.

You must learn to make a fist.

! When making a fist, never put your thumb inside your fingers. If your thumb is on the inside, it can be badly hurt, or even broken, when you punch.

KIHAP

The Korean term *kihap* is used to show that your mind and body are working together. During any powerful move, you must focus all your energy and determination. It helps if at the same time you give a short, explosive shout. As well as helping to give power, calling out the *kihap* gives you confidence, clearing your mind of fear and scaring your opponent.

PRACTICING STRAIGHT PUNCHING

Start in the sitting stance, with both fists palm-up.

1 Push your right fist forward to punch an imaginary opponent. Just before you punch, turn your fist palm-down.

2 Pull your right fist back, and at the same time push your left fist forward, so that your two fists pass each other in front of you.

3 Before your right arm reaches your body, turn it so that the palm is facing upward. At the same time, turn your left fist around into the punching position and make an imaginary punch. Remember to strike with your first two knuckles.

KNIFE-HAND AND PALM-HEEL

In tae kwon do, you can strike with the outside edge of your hand, called knife-hand or chop; with the inside edge, called ridge-hand; with the heel of your hand; or with the elbow.

For the palm-heel strike, bend your wrist back, hold your thumb against the side of your hand, and keep your fingers curved and away from the palm.

KICKING

Tae kwon do is famous for its kicks, which can be extremely powerful. They are particularly effective because legs are longer than arms, which means that kicks can reach farther than punches. Most tae kwon do kicks begin with the leg bent at the knee. The leg is then straightened to hit the target with different parts of the foot, but never the toes. It is important to keep the leg slightly bent, so as not to put too much strain on the knee.

You will probably learn to do front, round, side, and back kicks before you attempt the amazing jumping and flying tae kwon do kicks.

FRONT KICK

For this kick, *ap chagi,* start off in the ready **stance** and then slide your left foot forward. Bend your knees and keep your left fist up to guard your face.

1 Bring your right leg forward and raise your right foot, pulling the toes back.

2 When your right knee is high, thrust out your right leg, pushing your hips into the kick and keeping your toes pulled back. Imagine that you are hitting the target with the ball of your foot—the hard area just behind your toes. Keep your guard up during the kick.

BACK KICK

This kick, *dwi chagi*, involves turning your back on your opponent, so you should only use it as a surprise move or after another attacking technique.

Keep your eyes on your opponent as you lift your right foot and thrust it back in a straight line, heel first.

JUMPING FRONT KICK

Jumping kicks are made with both feet off the floor. To turn these into flying kicks, you have to take a few running steps, so that you move toward your opponent, and kick as you are in the air.

1 For the jumping front kick, first bring your left leg up high.

2 Then, as you snap that leg down again, lift your right knee and jump into the air.

3 Do a high front kick with your right leg.

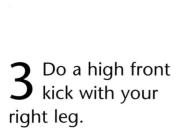

21

PATTERNS

All students of tae kwon do must learn a series of **patterns** or forms, called *poomse* in Korean. Practicing these patterns teaches you how to use the basic techniques of tae kwon do. The tae kwon do masters who developed the patterns made sure that they teach ways of dealing with attacks from all possible directions. The *poomse* also teach the proper way to carry out punches, kicks, and blocks. They are used in **grading** exams to test students.

The moves are like training **drills** with an imaginary opponent. At first you will learn them in individual stages, as shown in the sequence on this page. Then, with practice, you will be able to string them together smoothly. Your instructor will teach you how to use your whole body to deliver the power of each technique to a particular place.

DIFFERENT SYSTEMS

Different tae kwon do schools teach different systems of patterns. One traditional system is called *palgwe*. Many schools use a system authorized by the Korean Taekwondo Association, called *taegeuk*. The sequence shown here is made up of the first five movements of Form One in the *taegeuk* system, called *il-jang*.

IL-JANG

1 From the ready **stance,** turn to the left into a walking stance and perform an outer low block with the left arm.

2 Step forward one step with the right foot and punch with the right fist.

3 Pivot on your back foot as you turn clockwise to face the other way. Move your right leg to the front and perform a low block with the right arm.

4 Step forward one step with the left foot and punch with the left fist.

5 Turn to face forward again, go into a left-foot forward stance and perform an outer low block with the left arm.

The beginning of this sequence uses some of the basic techniques that we have seen earlier in the book. This first *taegeuk* continues with many more steps.

LEFT AND RIGHT

As in all martial arts, it is important that students can perform tae kwon do techniques from both sides of the body. Every student has a favorite side, often the same side as the hand with which they write. In training, you should concentrate particularly on your weaker side.

SPARRING

Sparring, or *kyorugi* in Korean, allows you to test the skills you have learned and practiced with a partner. At first all the sparring is prearranged, which means that both opponents agree beforehand what they are going to do. This makes it easier to move on to opposed contests later. It also allows you to learn how to use combinations of attacking and defensive techniques properly and get your timing right.

Different tae kwon do schools have varying attitudes toward sparring. Some allow only non-contact sparring, in which each strike is held back so that it does not quite reach the target. This is similar to the approach taken in **karate.** Other schools allow light contact, while some allow more contact. The amount of protective gear worn by the students depends on the type of sparring and the amount of contact they are allowed to make.

These young students are sparring without making any contact.

These more advanced students are allowed to make light contact as they spar with each other.

COOLING DOWN

It is important to cool down gently after any high-energy exercise such as tae kwon do. You can do this by jogging or walking, by breathing deeply, and by gently stretching, as you did when you warmed up. Some students like to cool down by doing some tae kwon do **pattern drills** to music.

BREAKING

Breaking techniques are used by advanced students to test and show the power of certain moves. At the opening ceremony of the 1988 Olympic Games, a tae kwon do **demonstration** team used their skill to break hundreds of boards. This is often what most people associate with tae kwon do. This is certainly not something that beginners should attempt, but you might see a demonstration from a tae kwon do master.

Expert students demonstrate an advanced breaking technique.

GRADING

When you join some tae kwon do clubs, you are given a license book. You use the license book to record your progress through the tae kwon do grades, all the way from beginner to expert. In other clubs you will receive certificates that record your progress through each level. Levels of skill are shown by different colored belts. The colors are based on a system of grades, called *kup*. You will start by wearing a white belt to show that you are at the tenth *kup*.

Your license book stays with you throughout your tae kwon do career.

BELT RANKS

There are five different belt colors covering the ten *kup* grades. When you have shown that you are on your way to the next color, a tab on the belt shows this. For example, you wear a yellow tab on your white belt when you are approaching the next color, yellow.

Kup grade	*Belt color*
10th	white
9th	white with yellow tab
8th	yellow
7th	yellow with green tab
6th	green
5th	green with blue tab
4th	blue
3rd	blue with red tab
2nd	red
1st	red with black tab

At each grade there is a different set of tae kwon do techniques to learn. To move up to the next grade, you will have to show that you can do them well. This will be tested in a **grading** exam, which may be given by your instructor. The exams vary, but you will probably have to perform basic techniques and certain **patterns,** as well as demonstrate your **sparring skills.**

It is normally expected that you have about 48 hours of training before you take each grading exam. If you train twice a week, there will be three to four months between each exam.

Tae kwon do students practice together for a grading exam.

BLACK BELT

The black belt is the top color, following the highest *kup* grade. It is split up into different *dans,* or degrees. These grades are usually awarded by special judges, and the student has to train for years between each *dan* grade, from the first *dan* to the very highest, ninth *dan.*

It usually takes about three years for a good tae kwon do student to gain a black belt, but this varies according to the rules of the club and how often the student trains. Grades are important and are to be respected, but you will notice that expert martial artists show complete respect for lower grades and beginners too. This respect is an important aspect of all the martial arts. You should never worry very much about which belt color you wear. Do your best, and you will progress at your own pace, whatever age you are when you begin.

A WORLD SPORT

Tae kwon do has become an important international sport. World championships are held every two years, and tae kwon do was one of just 28 sports represented at the 2000 Olympic Games. In international competition there are eight different weight divisions for both men and women, ranging from finweight—the lightest—to heavyweight.

Olympic and world championship tae kwon do follows the rules set by the World Taekwondo Federation (WTF), which allow full-contact blows and kicks. Contestants must wear special headgear, a chest protector, and forearm and shin padding. Every male contestant must wear a protective cup. Most competitors also wear mouthguards. The other major world organization is the International Taekwondo Federation (ITF), which allows only light contact.

RULES OF THE GAME

All tae kwon do contests take place on an 8¾-yard- (8-meter-) square blue elastic mat, surrounded by an outer, 13-yard- (12-meter-) square. Sometimes the area outside the contest area is red. Each match is controlled by a referee, but some tae kwon do clubs use three judges, some use four, and in Olympic matches there are six judges. A match is made up of three three-minute rounds.

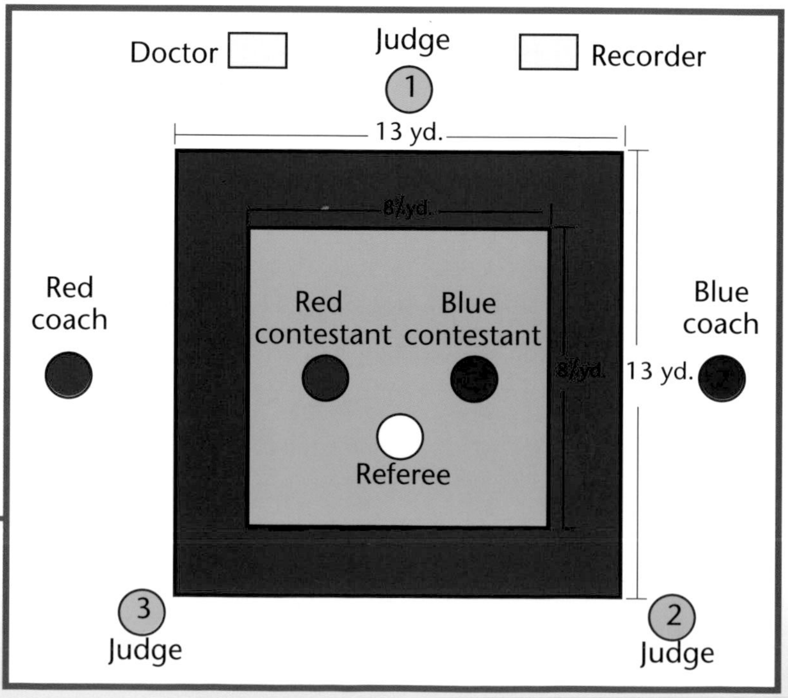

Doctor ▢   Judge ①   ▢ Recorder

13 yd.

8¾ yd.

Red coach ●

Red contestant ●   Blue contestant ●

Blue coach ●

8¾ yd.   13 yd.

○ Referee

③ Judge   ② Judge

This diagram shows one possible layout for an official match area.

28

One of the two contestants has blue marks on his *dobok* and is called *chung,* and the other has red marks and is known as *hong.* Points are scored for proper blows to the target areas on the opponent. These are on the front and sides of the body above the waist for hand and foot techniques. Foot strikes are also allowed to the head. Points are taken away for fouls, such as grabbing, holding, or pushing. Three penalty points result in the contestant being disqualified. If a contestant is knocked down by a proper attack, and has not recovered by the time the referee counts to ten, he or she loses the match.

If a match ends in a tie, the referee decides which contestant should be the winner. Any kick technique is considered better than a punch, a jumping kick is better than a standing kick, and a **counter-attack** is better than an initial attack.

A total of 550 contestants from 66 different countries took part in the world championships in Edmonton, Canada, in 1999. Korea won 9 of the 16 gold medals. Prizes for the best fighting spirit went to Jordan, Brazil, and Sweden.

KOREAN WORDS

To say these Korean words, sound them out the way they are written here.

Korean word	Meaning	Korean word	Meaning
ap chagi	front kick	*il-jang*	first pattern in the *taegeuk* series
apkoobi	walking stance		
arae makki	down or low block	*kihap*	explosive shout that gives power
choochoom soegi	sitting stance		
choonbi	ready or first stance	*kup*	grade
chung	blue (contestant)	*kyorugi*	sparring
dobok	tae kwon do outfit	*kyungye*	bow
dojang	training hall	*momtong makki*	inner or inside block
dwi chagi	back kick	*palgwe*	series of patterns
dwit koobi	L stance	*poomse*	patterns or forms
eolgol makki	rising or upper block	*subak*	early form of tae kwon do
hong	red (contestant)		
hwarang	flower of youth	*taegeuk*	series of patterns
		taekkyon	early form of Korean combat

GLOSSARY

aggressive   forceful or hostile

counter-attack   attack that replies to an attack by an opponent

drill   repeating something so you learn it well

grading   marking a performance so that a student goes into a particular ability group

judo   Japanese martial art that uses throwing and grappling techniques

karate   Japanese martial art that uses both hands and feet to make high-energy punches, strikes, and kicks

kung fu   general term for all Chinese martial arts

pattern   set of moves that is learned as a training drill

senior grade   experienced tae kwon do student who is at a higer level or grade

spar   to have a practice contest, sometimes with the moves agreed beforehand

stance   position of the body, with the feet in a special place and the arms held in a special way

MORE BOOKS TO READ

Lloyd, Bryant. *Martial Arts...The History.* Vero Beach, Fla.: Rourke Press, Inc., 1998.

Randall, Pamela. *Tae Kwon Do.* New York: Rosen Publishing Group, Inc., 1999.

Yates, Keith D., and Bryan Robbins. *Tae Kwon Do for Kids.* New York: Sterling Publishing Co., 1999.

TAKING IT FURTHER

American Taekwondo Association (ATA)
6210 Baseline Road
Little Rock, AR 72209
Telephone: (501) 568-2821

International Taekwondo Federation (ITF)
Drau Gasse 3
1210 Vienna, Austria

United States Taekwon-Do Federation (USTF)
6801 W. 117th Ave. E-5
Broomfield, CO 80020
Telephone: (303) 466-4963

United States Taekwondo Union (USTU)
One Olympic Plaza, Suite 405
Colorado Springs, CO 80909
Telephone: (719) 578-4632

World Taekwondo Federation (WTF)
635 Yuksamdong Kangnamku
Seoul 135-080, Korea

INDEX